Contents

A Word From
Alex Hooper-Hodson

Being a teenager is the most exciting time of your life. Your generation has almost unlimited choices compared to girls in the past. You have been born into an age of revolutionary advances in technology, medicine and culture. Because of this, girls of your generation can pursue any ambition they want to – personally and professionally.

Over the decade that I've been an agony uncle I've received thousands of letters from teen girls on everything from bullying, shyness and relationships to gaining confidence, improving your self image and managing social media. But I've discovered that while the names and situations may change, there are in fact just 52 key problems that can or do affect teen girls' lives. So by collecting together sample letters in this book, I hope to provide a unique perspective for teen girls everywhere. For those problems that feel just too tough to deal with on your own, I've provided a list of help agencies on pages 94-95.

As an agony uncle, my job is to listen to and offer advice on all sorts of problems, but I don't want you to go away from this book thinking that your next few years are going to be a trial and that every one of these 52 problems MUST happen to you. I have included each of them in this book as a guide so that you have the knowledge and tools you need to manage them effectively and then go on to enjoy what really matters – being a happy and fulfilled teenage girl!

I think teenagers rarely get the credit they deserve for how well they cope with this stage of life! For managing so well, you have my admiration and best wishes.

Alex Hooper-Hodson

Chapter One

It's Your Body & Your Life

Alex says

This growing up thing...

It could happen today, it could happen tomorrow or maybe it already happened to you last week; the morning when you wake up and realise that something is different. Tell-tale signs have been building up for months, but now you've finally realised where they were leading. Something deep inside you has changed forever; you're no longer the little girl who let her mum choose her clothes for her and who happily accepted the world around her with a smile. Suddenly your head is full of doubts; what kind of image are you presenting to the outside world? What do people think of you? What's the right way to act and be cool?

How has none of this really mattered to you before, you ask yourself, while you notice that your skin has decided to break out into spots! And what about the adults in your life? Why don't they understand how much your life has changed? There are boys and girls out there you are interested in being friends with. You want to stand out from the crowd — if you want to dye your hair or wear black eyeliner to school then what's the big deal?

Some girls like wearing high-street fashions and being part of the crowd. Others want to push their identity further and follow groups that prefer dramatic hairstyles, clothes and make up. Whatever look you choose, the important thing is that YOU feel comfortable doing it.

Coming to terms with all the changes that are going on in your life can be tricky – even with the most supportive parents in the world! The truth is that while it's hard for you, it can also be hard on parents or the other adults in your life, as they can take time to adjust too!

During your teen years it's common to have moments of self-doubt when looking in the mirror, but in this chapter you will see how other girls have tackled issues of body image at this crucial time in life. While my advice can't always make the problem go away, hopefully it can help you to cope with it a little bit better...

Why don't my parents understand me? This is who I am!

I turned 14 last month and my best friend suggested giving me a makeover. So we arranged a sleepover during which she dyed my hair with a reddish tint and lent me some of her clothes and make up to finish off the look. Her mum is really supportive of her and will buy her any clothes she wants. She even buys her make up and hair dye.

I thought my parents would be excited by my makeover but my dad just frowned and my mum told me off for not asking permission. It seems so unfair that they reacted in this way. Why can't they be more like my friend's mum and just be happy for me? They just don't understand that I'm not trying to upset them — I'm just trying to express myself and be me!

Chitra, 14

Alex says

I sympathise with you on this as I felt the same at times, but it's important to realise that not all families are the same. They all have different outlooks and rules and your friend's mum's relaxed attitude to her daughter's appearance is personal to her and her family. Remember: it was only very recently that your parents saw you as their little girl. I know this makeover is your way of showing them that you are growing up, but it may take some time for them to adjust to the idea so be patient.

Just as some of the changes you are going through are confusing and scary for you, they can be the same for your parents. Eventually they will get used to the idea that you are growing up and making decisions without their input. However, if you want them to come round to your point of view, introduce change gradually rather than all at once — and talk it through first so it isn't such a shock. Small changes here and there are a lot easier to get used to and will help your parents to see that you've put some thought into your actions...

It took my mum a while to get used to my new image but in the end she did. Now we go out together to choose clothes!
Seren, 13

Parents are more likely to accept small changes at the beginning. Try doing your hair first and get them used to that before moving on to clothes. Good luck!
Deanne, 14

My friend's mum banned make up, colouring hair or wearing mini skirts. Now she's a bit older her mum has cooled off. You just have to be patient.
Rhian, 14

2 Is there any way to get rid of spots once and for all?

Help! I'm always in the middle of a spot crisis. As soon as I get rid of one on my face, another appears to take its place. I feel like I'm fighting a losing battle with my skin. I never know if the spot cream I'm buying is actually helping or if I'm just throwing my money away. Is there a spot treatment on the market that actually works? If so, where can I get it?

Bea, 13

Alex says

During puberty all teenagers get spots thanks to the cocktail of hormones that are surging around their bodies. These hormones make the skin produce greater amounts of sebum, which is an oily substance that protects the skin from drying out. Hair follicles then become blocked by the sebum. At the same time, hormonal changes will alter the levels of acid in your skin, encouraging the growth of bacteria, and when this infects a blocked hair follicle, a spot (pustule) or acne (nodule) occurs. Keeping your skin clean is a first step in combating spots but luckily there are a number of 'over the counter' spot treatments that can also help. Make sure you buy spot treatments containing either benzoyl peroxide or salicylic acid. If you've tried these products for at least 6 weeks and your skin still hasn't responded then see your GP, as there are a range of prescribed treatments that can help get rid of spots, including antibiotics.

3 Why am I the only one not to have started my period?

I've been having a really tough time at school lately. All the other girls in my class have already started their periods and aren't shy about letting me know. It's really horrible being the odd one out. Could there be something wrong with me? What's the RIGHT age to get your period — and is there a way to speed it up?

Emily, 13

Alex says

Being the odd one out at school isn't a pleasant experience, particularly when it's your body that's the issue. But I want to reassure you that it's perfectly normal not to have started your periods by now. In fact, there is no 'right' age to start. Some girls start as young as 8 or 9, while others don't start until they're 16 or 17. The majority of girls find they begin between the ages of 11 and 14 so there's no reason to suspect you're a late bloomer. Unfortunately there's no way to speed things up. I know it feels like you're being singled out, but nature will take its course — so relax and rest assured that it will happen.

 DO Relax — nature will take its course.

DON'T Compare yourself to other girls — our bodies are all different.

4. I'm not too young to dress up but mum says no!

> I'm 15 years old and want to dress up when I go out, but my mum has definite ideas about how I should look. She hates me wearing heels and short skirts. As for make up, she would prefer it if I didn't wear any at all! All my friends wear fashionable stuff but she says that dressing too old for my age will attract the 'wrong attention'. Why can't she understand that I'm not a child anymore?

Olivia, 15

Alex says

This is a tricky problem, but your mum's attitude stems from her concern that if you 'dress up' then some boys may see you as sexually available. Some of her ideas may seem old-fashioned to you, but remember she was a teenager once and probably had the same arguments with her mother! Compromise might be the best solution here. Sit down and talk to your mum and try to work out some guidelines that will might work for both of you. Take skirt length — if she wants your skirt length to be below the knee and you want it above, why not agree to meet exactly in the middle? The great thing about negotiating is that you get something of what you want. Your mum will respect your level-headed approach to dealing with things and may even ease up on her rules a little. But don't expect miracles overnight. You will need to be patient as these things can take time.

It happened to me

My mum was always really strict about make up. I wasn't allowed to wear it out of the house, even though all my friends did. I felt as if she was treating me like a baby. I started to put on make up in secret at friends' houses before we went out, but I couldn't apply eyeliner very well and so my mum found out what I was doing. She got mad at me and said I looked a real mess! I got upset and tried to explain to her that I felt like the odd one out. Funnily enough, she actually stopped to listen to me and then said that if I wanted she would give me some tips on how to apply it so that I didn't look as if I was wearing too much. We had a great couple of afternoons looking at make up tutorials together on YouTube and then trying them out. Thanks to the tutorials I know now how to apply make up and what suits me best. It feels like mum and I have bonded over this and our relationship has improved. In fact, we're getting on really well at the moment, and in future, instead of banging heads I think we will communicate much better.

Amy, 15

5 Will a nose piercing really ruin my life?

I want to get my nose pierced but my dad has given a definite no. He thinks having a nose piercing will ruin my life, but I think he's being old-fashioned. Lots of girls have their noses pierced these days. They don't mind me having my ears pierced so what's the difference? How can I get them to see things from my point of view?

Tilly, 14

Alex says

To you, an ear piercing and a nose piercing are similar but that's not the problem here. It may seem old-fashioned but social attitudes to piercings differ. Schools and many employers tend not to have very liberal views on body piercings. Ears are usually fine; eyebrows, noses, tongues, lips and so on usually aren't. It's likely that your school will not tolerate a nose piercing and future employers may see it as 'unprofessional' and choose not to employ you. Piercings can be removed but remember that they leave holes or scars that can last forever. When you're older it will be your decision, but by then it will also be clearer what's at stake. Until that time, if you really can't hang on I suggest buying clip-on jewellery that gives exactly the same effect as a piercing.

 DO Think about the future – you only get one body.

 DON'T Rush into things as piercings leave scars.

6 I'm getting teased for having hairy legs. Help!

All the girls at school have been teasing me for having hairy legs. I know that women usually shave their legs but I have no idea where to begin. Do I need shaving foam? What kind of razor do I use? What direction do I shave – up or down? I know I should ask my mum but it's too embarrassing! If you could tell me the basics it would really help.

Keri, 14

Alex says

Don't feel pressured into shaving your legs just because others have made you feel humiliated about something that is completely normal. Not every woman shaves nor is there any law saying they must do. Some women feel that body hair is normal and choose to keep it, while others choose to shave it off. The choice is yours. But why don't you go ahead and talk to your mum (or older sister or aunt) first about what's been happening and discuss with them whether shaving is the best option for you or not (there are a multitude of ways to remove body hair should you choose to get rid of it). The good thing about asking for someone's help is that they'll be able to advise you on what to do and show you the right way to remove the hair on your legs (should you wish to!). Good luck.

7 My breasts are too big – what can I do?

> I am the only girl in my class to have big breasts. They started growing when I was about 9 and have been getting bigger ever since. Some days I feel like everyone's forgotten there's more to me than just my boobs. Girls always tell me that they're jealous and I'm always catching boys looking at them. I wish there was a way to make them smaller so that I don't stand out so much!

Andi, 13

Alex says

It may seem like you've been singled out by nature but this is not the case. Puberty affects girls at different rates and you happen to be an early developer. Pretty soon the rest of the class will more or less catch up with you and what seems 'big' today will probably seem standard and you won't feel so self-conscious. The boys will probably go on being boys (boys tend to mature later than girls, hence the embarrassment) and your friends will feel less envious. In the meantime, make sure you get professionally fitted for the right sized bra. You can get a proper bra fitting in many department stores and it's not an embarrassing process at all. The correct size of bra can do a number of things for your body confidence, including help to shape and minimise your breast size so that you feel much happier with the way you look.

Chapter Two

Get To Know Your Own Mind

Who do you think you are?

 This chapter looks at the problems and anxieties that can affect your thinking during your teenage years.

It's well known that this time can be full of emotional highs and lows. Often this is blamed on 'hormones' as if the thoughts and feelings you are experiencing are the product of some wayward chemicals surging through your body.

Hormones are not only responsible for physical changes such as weight gain and spots (which can make you feel gloomy) but along with your experiences and your environment, account for the fundamental changes in the way you will start to think about yourself. Here are some of the issues that affect the majority of teens:

The search for identity Part of the growing up process is about discovering who you are and where you 'fit' into the wider world. This can be influenced by all sorts of things such as your personal experiences, your family's beliefs and ideals, the influence of your siblings, friends and teachers, and of course your cultural background.

The need for independence After spending the last 12 or 13 years happily relying on mum and dad you may suddenly want your privacy and find you are craving some independence. It might take parents a little while to get used to this – after all they've been there for you every day since the day you were born!

Peer pressure Your peers are people who are the same age as you and in the same social group, such as your school friends. Giving in to peer pressure is when you let the views or opinions of these people influence your actions negatively (although peer pressure can work positively, too). This might mean that they suggest you do something you wouldn't normally do, or it might mean that they change the way you feel about yourself on the inside.

Self-esteem As we grow up each one of us builds a mental picture of ourselves, often referred to as a 'self image'. Much of this self image is influenced by the interactions we have with other people and our life experiences. Self-esteem is how worthy we feel inside and out (so includes self image). As we grow up some of us develop a greater sense of self-esteem, while for others the opposite happens and they form a negative view of themsevles (low self esteem).

Communication and social media Facebook, Twitter, Tumblr and any other social networking sites and apps and includes instant and text messaging, smartphone use and online gaming such as X-Box, Playstation or Wii. At no other time in history has the development of the teenage mind been so affected by social networking as it is today. Read on to find out more!

8 How can I become more confident in social situations?

> I get really nervous in social situations. The problem is worse when I'm around large groups of strangers. I get butterflies in my stomach, my mouth goes dry and I always need to go to the bathroom! It's only a problem I've had for the last year, but it doesn't show any sign of going away. I wish there was some way that I could boost my confidence so that I didn't feel so self-conscious all the time. Can you help?

Ellie, 15

Alex says

What's happening to you is a very common problem and affects everyone at one time or another. But by worrying about your symptoms (like noticing your heart is beating faster or that your mouth is a bit dry) you can make them worse, so try to relax. When you notice your stress, try relaxing your shoulders and take a few deep breaths to calm yourself. In a social setting, this means telling yourself that you are excited to meet new people and reminding yourself to be strong. Remember, most other people are just as nervous as you are – they simply hide it better! Take the focus off yourself by asking questions of some of the new people you are meeting. People like to asked about themselves and this is so much better for you than concentrating on your own reactions. If your anxiety gets worse and is stopping you from getting on with your life, it's worth visiting your GP to see if counselling or therapy can help you.

9 I'm being teased on Facebook!

When I turned 13 and was allowed a Facebook account I really hoped it would help me make some new friends, but it's had the opposite effect! One of the girls at school started to leave nasty status updates about me, which she tagged me in. At first the other girls would just 'like' the updates but now they are all joining in saying nasty things about me that are not true! Please help me, I don't know what to do.

Jaswinder, 13

Alex says

What you're describing is cyberbullying. And just as we cannot tolerate bullies in the real world, social media is no different. In many ways it can feel worse than real-life bullying as it's there 24/7 — and it can invade your life at home as well as at school. There are two ways to tackle this: either think about deleting your Facebook account or take action. To take action, start by letting your parents and your school know what is happening to you. Then block all the people involved in the bullying (you can do this in your Facebook settings). This way they won't be able to 'tag' you into their updates or see your page and you won't be able to see them. If it continues via others, put out a status that says you will be taking action on anyone who bullies you online. Facebook does not tolerate bullying and will remove bullying content and even disable the account of anyone who attacks another. The best way to report it is via Facebook's report links.

10 I always seem to have something to stress about. Please help!

Since I turned 13 last year I always seem to have something to worry about. I used to be the most carefree person in the world, but this year it feels like everything has changed for the worse. I stress about schoolwork, my parents, my health, my friends' problems, boys, and a million other things! My mum suggested I write down the things that I'm worried about to help me to work through them, and I've taken to making lists so that I don't forget to do things. The problem is, now I make dozens of lists. I know this behaviour isn't normal and I'm starting to scare myself. I don't understand how life has become so much more stressful over the last year when before my life seemed so happy and straightforward?

Kate, 13

Stress is the body's response to physical, mental, or emotional changes or situations. This means it can result from external factors (e.g. events, environment) or from internal factors (e.g. expectations, attitudes, feelings). Stress also occurs in response to situations that are perceived as being difficult to handle or threatening. Some of us are also more prone to stress due to our personality and even the way our own family handle stress. At 13 there's an awful lot of pressure placed on you from school, peers and family and in your case I think you have started to look at these things in an exaggerated way. You can't control every aspect of the world around you – especially other people and the decisions they make. At some point you have to simply let go and accept that certain things will carry on as they are, whether you worry about them or not! Your mum sounds supportive so why not sit down and tell her exactly how you feel. If your feelings of stress become overwhelming then it may be good to speak to a counsellor who will help you process the demands of the world around you.

I used to get really stressed until I talked to my school counsellor. She suggested I start a diary to help organise my schoolwork.
Leah, 14

It may be that you have taken on too much. Let your friends look after their own problems and take care of yourself for a bit.
Sara, 13

It can help to make a list but having too many things on your list can stress you out, so keep it simple!
Tanya, 15

Counselling really helped me. I only went for a few sessions but it put things in perspective. Life can be stressful but talking about it to someone can make it seem much easier.
Lorna, 15

11

Please help, I hate my life a little bit more every day...

I'm writing to you because my emotions are out of control and I don't know what to do. Some days I feel fine, but others I feel like everything in my life is awful and there's absolutely nothing I can do about it. It started last year when some girls from my school started to bully me on YouTube. They would post awful videos where they would say some really nasty things about me. It got really bad until my mum found out and called my school. Ever since then my moods have been really up and down and I've hardly wanted to leave the house. Now whenever something bad happens it feels like it's building up to something even worse. I'm worried there's something wrong with my head and I don't know where to turn for help. I've tried talking to my mum but she just tells me it's normal 'teenage mood swings'.

Dana, 15

Alex says

What you're experiencing are the after-effects of being bullied. Many victims of bullying suffer from crushed confidence levels long after the bullying has stopped. They find that they can't cope and/or panic when anything upsetting happens to them. What you need to do is talk to your mum again and also contact one of the bullying helplines (see the Get Connnected! section on pages 94-95) for advice and support. It's vital to do this now because if your feelings are not addressed properly they can grow and turn into something more overwhelming and serious, like depression. Right now it may feel as if your despair will never lift, but with the correct help and support you will start to feel better and more hopeful about things.

> I was getting bullied every day at school. It got so bad I stopped going. I felt like I couldn't talk to anyone. In the end it was talking to my teacher that turned things around for me.
> Cate, 14

> You MUST talk to someone about what's going on. Also focus on things that make you feel happy and good about yourself.
> Tia, 15

> Your self-esteem has taken a bashing and you need to build yourself back up. Contact one of the bullying helplines now and get some professional advice.
> Viola, 13

 **DO** Seek help and support.

 **DON'T** Let your feelings build.

When Everything Hurts: Teen Depression

Your teens are a time of intense change that can play havoc with your emotions. It's normal to have moody days, perhaps due to hormones or because you've reached a certain stage in your menstrual cycle (periods). Gloomy weather or the prospect of a weekend packed full with homework essays can also, at times, make you feel pretty low!

Often, feeling a bit depressed is linked to something specific. Perhaps you've argued with your mum, fallen out with your best friend, failed an exam or the boy you like hasn't noticed you. At these times you can feel so miserable that you start to wonder if things will ever get better. But it's important to remember that these feelings will pass — maybe tomorrow, or in a week or in a few months. To help yourself, talk to a close friend you can trust and get the sad and negative feelings out of your head. Be kind to yourself, reassure yourself that things will get better and bolster your confidence until you start to feel good about life again. These low and gloomy feelings are real, but they are not signs of depression, and they don't call for a trip to your GP unless you feel like this all the time.

Of course, teens can get depressed just like anyone else, but you need to remember that people who are ill with depression have serious symptoms of emptiness and despair. They are unable to look on the bright side, often can't sleep (or sleep too much), eat too little, or binge on food all day, lose all track of time, can't concentrate and cannot become interested in anything. The good news is that all but the most serious depressions can be helped by taking regular exercise, eating well, going to sleep at a regular time and challenging your negative thoughts by talking to someone you trust.

Talking helps because the more you talk through your problems (this can be with a parent or counsellor) the easier it is to start to unravel your feelings, make sense of them and find a way to get beyond what's causing your depression and sadness. If your problems don't ease by talking about them then you need to see your GP. This is especially important if you are harming yourself or thinking of harming yourself. This in itself is a big warning sign that you need to take action and seek professional help through your GP.

In other cases, depression can develop and become a 'syndrome' such as social anxiety, substance disorders (drug addiction) or bi-polar disorder (manic depression). These types of depression need to be treated with a mixture of therapy and, in some cases, medication. Bi-polar disorder is characterised by extreme mood swings. The sufferer may feel excessively low and exhausted on one day, and 'high' and 'overactive' the next. During these periods behaviour can seem exaggerated, making little sense to family or friends. Bi-polar disorder is a serious condition and qualifies as a serious depression.

If you or anyone you know shows signs of either depression or any of the disorders described above, then the next step is to talk to family about it and visit your GP. With the help of a type of therapy and counselling it's possible to alleviate many depressive conditions.

It happened to me

I was the last girl in my class to get my period. I didn't start until I was nearly 16 and I was also the tallest in the class. Most of my so-called friends started their periods around 11 or 12 and became interested in boys. They teased me because I wasn't into the idea of boys at all. Around this time my parents divorced. Having been really good with my schoolwork, I just couldn't hack it and when it got to the stage of not handing in any homework the teachers got really angry with me. I felt terrible all the time. I spent a lot of my time in my room. I started cutting my arms. It's odd but it was the only thing that helped with the pain I was feeling. But one day mum saw my arms when I was coming out of the shower. She took me to our GP who checked me out physically and then he referred me to a therapist, someone who specialised in treating self-harm and depression. It took time but I'm enjoying life a lot more now, I'm coping well with sixth form college and most importantly, I wouldn't even consider hurting myself again.

Ophelia, 17

12 My parents insist I'm in bed by 9 o'clock!

Sian, 13

> My parents think that 9pm is an acceptable time for me to be in bed. I want them to understand that I'm not a little kid anymore. All my friends' parents let them stay up and they even get to watch late night TV! Mum and dad say it doesn't matter what other families do and say I need a proper night's sleep. If a 'proper night's sleep' is so important then why aren't they in bed by 9pm too?

Alex says

I'm afraid your parents are right when they say that you need a good night's sleep. Teenagers need about 9 hours sleep a night for them to function at their best. Older adults need far less (6+ hours). If you're talking about school nights then it is essential you get enough rest – it's no good if you end up nodding off in class! Different families have their own rules but the best way to get your parents to consider your viewpoint is to put your ideas across calmly and not to make demands. I doubt they'll change their view on staying up late on school nights just yet, but see if they will relax the rules a little for the weekend.

 DO Be calm and try to compromise.

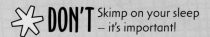 **DON'T** Skimp on your sleep – it's important!

13 My parents don't even have Facebook accounts!

It's like my parents and I live in different centuries. They don't even have Facebook! I talk on Skype to my friends in Japan, use Facebook and Twitter to keep up with what people are up to and Instagram to post and check out interesting pictures. When my mum asks me what bands I like I'd be happy to send her playlists from Spotify or Deezer but she doesn't know what they are. It's the same with satellite TV and YouTube – they usually dismiss them as 'rubbish'. I don't expect them to change overnight but I wish they were a bit more 'connected' as I think it would improve our relationship. What do you think?

Georgina, 13

Alex says

The key to getting your parents to tech up is to emphasise the positives of new technology not bombard them with tech jargon and ideas they haven't yet grasped. Step one would be to teach them to send a text message, then build up to things like email and social networking. One great way to get them to embrace the online world would be to create a Facebook profile page for both of them and link them up to their friends so they can see how easy it is and how useful and fun it is. There's also a great site called Teach Parents Tech (www.teachparentstech. org) where they can watch videos that show tech beginners how to do a variety of things from share photos to upgrade their browser. Above all don't get so exasperated with them. They spent years teaching you how to do everything from eat to walk and read, now it's your turn to return the favour.

My mum said she was too old for FB. So one day I made her an account and showed her the basics. She found that all her friends were on there and now she uses it every day!
Bryony, 16

I wouldn't mind if my parents weren't using social media. It's just each to his or her own isn't it?
Lucy, 14

My dad was always suspicious of social media, but since my uncle moved to New Zealand, he's realised how awesome Skype can be to keep in touch!
Dannielle, 13

14. I get so angry with my parents!

My parents never seem to see my point of view on anything! I get so angry with them. They make jokes about me being a 'typical teen' but it's not funny. I feel so trapped by all their silly rules. Sometimes I feel a bit out of control. Once I smashed up my bedroom and another time I lashed out at my dad. I feel like I hate my parents sometimes!

Chloe, 14

Alex says

No matter how angry it might make you feel, you don't have the right to hurt your parents or to smash up their home (even if it's your room). Next time you get angry like this you need to take a deep breath, walk out of the room and count to 10 in your head. Then take another deep breath and compose yourself. Unfortunately, your anger is only demonstrating to them that you still have a lot of growing up to do. They would respect your opinions more if you challenged them calmly and rationally, and discussed finding a compromise. Work on getting your anger under control, but if it keeps on taking hold then speak to your mum, aunt or a trusted teacher. Serious anger issues can be dealt with by specialist counsellors who will be able to help you.

 **DO** Take a deep breath!

 **DON'T** Lose your cool...

15 I'm afraid someone might hurt me!

My family often watches the news while having dinner in the evening. It always seems to be full of terrible things going on all over the world. Recently I've been getting more and more scared of going out on my own because something might happen to me. It sometimes seems like there are terrorists, muggers and violent criminals everywhere – even in our small town! My dad always says not to talk to strangers. I know this is good advice but I'm worried about all kinds of things happening to me!

Hannah, 13

Alex says

It's true that the news is full of awful events and terrorism has been in the news a lot in the last decade or so, but try to keep your fears in perspective. Statistically speaking, it's unlikely that you will ever be involved in a terrorist attack. If news programmes frighten you, suggest to your family that you don't watch them over dinner. It's one thing to be street aware and another to let these fears overtake your life. Of course, street crime is more of a serious concern. When you're out on the street keep your wits about you. Don't stare at people on the street and try not to meet a stranger's gaze. Don't walk around alone at night. Stick to well-lit areas and don't take shortcuts. Keep your mobile or iPod well hidden. Act confidently and look like you know where you are going. If you think someone is following you, head immediately for the nearest shop or well populated area and phone the police. Don't be afraid to ask for help if you need it!

16 I can't stop thinking about death and dying!

I'm terrified of dying. I lie awake at night trying to imagine what it would feel like to die. I worry about whether there is an afterlife. I worry about all my family and friends dying. Obviously I've known about death since I was a little girl, but I'm sure it's not normal to think about it all the time. Can you help me?

Nicky, 14

Alex says

Worrying about death is quite normal and a part of life that we all go through at one time or another. However, try to see that focusing on death and imagining that you're going to die and lose all your loved ones is futile. It doesn't help, and it doesn't make the present time very enjoyable for you. On the one hand, don't be afraid to express your fears to trusted people in your life as I am sure many of your friends will have gone through the same process. At the same time, work on taking the focus off these negative thoughts and concentrate on living now! Join a sports club or theatre group, start a new hobby or just hang out with friends doing something you all enjoy and you will soon forget thoughts of death and dying and start enjoying life again.

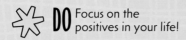 **DO** Focus on the positives in your life!

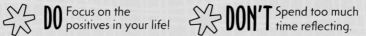 **DON'T** Spend too much time reflecting.

17

My granddad died and I can't stop crying.

Last month my granddad passed away. I loved him so much and always looked forward to spending time with him. He's the first person that I've known who has died. When my mum told me it was a really big shock. I just couldn't believe that wouldn't see him again. I started crying on the way to school the other day. My dad said to let it out and then he cried too. It was really sad. Can you help?

Desi, 14

Alex says

We all deal with loss in different ways. Some people bottle things up, while others express their feelings openly. There is no 'right' way to deal with loss; grief is a natural process and it will take time for you deal with what has happened. It's early days for you yet, so try to open up and talk to your dad and the other people you love and trust about how you are feeling. It would help both you and your dad to remember the good times you had with your granddad. In time, perhaps frame some special pictures of him to keep around the house or keep an album of photos that will remind you of special times you spent together. You can't change what's happened, but you should try to support each other so you don't feel so alone in your sadness.

18 I'm worried I've become anorexic!

Since about the age of 12 I've never liked my body. I spend hours looking in the mirror, obsessing over every tiny detail. Are my thighs fat? Are my arms flabby? Do I look as good as the other girls at school? Are they skinnier than me? I started dieting and recently it's become more extreme. My calorie-counting has really got intense. I've been living on salad and fizzy drinks for several weeks now and I'm really scared I might be anorexic. I don't know where to go for help.

Pippa, 15

Alex says

Eating disorders like anorexia are very serious conditions. Your salad and fizzy drink diet is not providing you with the nutrients you need to fuel your body and you are in serious danger of becoming ill. You must confide in someone you trust, immediately. An appointment with your GP will get you a referral to a specialist who is trained to deal with eating disorders. The good news is that eating disorders are all treatable and people can recover from them and go on to live healthy lives. You should also check out the websites listed in the Get Connected! section on pages 94-95 for help with eating disorders. But the first step for you is to be honest with your family — and take action now!

 DO Confide in someone you trust.

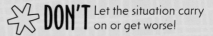 **DON'T** Let the situation carry on or get worse!

19

I make myself sick after meals because I can't stand to feel full.

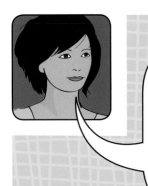

I used to be overweight and was really self-conscious about it. Then I discovered that if I made myself sick after eating, the problem went away. I still got to enjoy the taste of the food but I didn't put on any weight, and in fact I started to lose weight. The problem is I can't stand to feel full anymore and have to make myself sick. I've started having really bad stomach pains and have even fainted a few times. Please help!

Mei, 15

Alex says

It's very brave of you to open up about this and I urge you to be as honest with your parents now. The condition you describe is called bulimia nervosa (or bulimia for short) and it is a recognised eating disorder. It can start as an extreme way to control your weight, but as you've discovered it ends up being addictive and is bad for your health. You are risking lifelong stomach disorders, gastric reflux and tooth decay from it. Like other eating problems, bulimia can occur due to deep-rooted issues and part of beating it can be to tackle the issue itself. The first step is to visit your GP who will refer you to a specialist who deals with eating disorders. Good luck and be brave. You have made an enormous step by admitting you have a problem already – don't stop now. You should also check out the websites listed in the Get Connected! section on pages 94-95 for help with eating disorders.

37

20 I eat to cheer myself up but it just makes things worse!

Ever since I can remember I've been bullied about my weight. It really hurts because I've tried so hard to lose weight. The worst thing is that when people say nasty things about me it makes me want to hide in my room and eat even more to make myself feel better. My mum is overweight too and so doesn't see it as a problem. I've tried asking her to cook healthy meals but it's not her thing. Everything she cooks is either deep-fried or served with chips. She also fills the cupboards with cakes, sweets, chocolate and crisps. I know that if she supported me just a little bit more I'd have a better chance at beating this. I don't know how to convince my mum that there is a problem. In my dreams I am a size zero but I know that will never happen.

Gill, 15

Alex says

The media encourages us all to admire body shapes like size zero, which is both unhelpful and unrealistic. What you need to do is be very honest with your mum. Tell her that you're unhappy about your weight and also that you're being bullied about it. It would help this situation if you or your mum spoke to your school to get their support on bullying and how to stamp it out. Next, I suggest you go to your GP together so you can get some advice on how to change your diet. The doctor will measure your Body Mass Index (BMI). This is a score that can let you know if you do have a weight problem and if so how serious it is. Your doctor will also be able to talk to your mum about the impact that the wrong kind of food can have on health, and give you some diet sheets and practical strategies to help you lose weight safely and effectively. If your mum sees that there is a real issue here, then she's less likely to fill the cupboards with junk food and help you to start eating and feeling more healthy. Hope it helps!

The image the media wants us to aspire to is nonsense. If you want to change the way you look for health reasons then great, but don't be pressurised by a so-called ideal weight 'size zero'!
Jules, 16

Everyone at school used to call me names for having big legs. I used to feel so much pressure to be thin. In the end I learned to appreciate my good points and just ignore them.
Polly, 13

Your body changes so much as you go through your teens anyway. The perfect body doesn't exist. You'll always find fault with yourself unless you figure this out.
Lola, 15

If you get your mum to help you then things will become so much easier.
Anjali, 13

21 What's the big deal about GCSEs?

> Mum is always telling me I have to work hard at school but I find a lot of my lessons boring. I'd rather be hanging out with my friends than learning about stuff that happened a zillion years ago. Mum says if I don't pay attention in class I won't pass my GCSEs but I don't really care. What's so important about them anyway?

Lisa, 15

Alex says

School can seem a bit tiresome and irrelevant in your teenage years, particularly when you feel there's a world out there waiting to be explored. But there is a very good reason to pay attention and take it seriously. The subjects taught in schools are designed to give you the knowledge and qualifications you're going to need to get the sort of jobs you'll want in the future. Almost ALL modern careers require GCSEs! The time for a job will come quicker than you can imagine, and if you've put in the hard work at school you will give yourself more options for what to do when you leave. It's true that you can go back and re-sit exams later, but it's likely you'll be out of step with your friends who are all moving on to college. My advice to you on this would be: just get your head down and get your exams!

22 Recently I have no confidence in myself. What can I do?

Tori, 15

> At my old school I felt good about who I was. My family made me feel great and I didn't give a thought to how I looked – I was happy with myself. Since I joined my new school a group of girls has been calling me names and making jokes about my body. It happens every day and it's beginning to make me feel small. It's started to affect my schoolwork and even my confidence in sports. I know I shouldn't let their opinions get to me but they do. I can't help it. I feel like there must be some truth in it or why would they say these horrible things?

Alex says

This type of verbal bullying should be tackled straight away, since it's having such a detrimental effect on your confidence and self-esteem. Report the girls' behaviour to a teacher at school and let him or her know what is going on; no one deserves this kind of daily abuse. Then every morning when you wake up, look in the mirror and focus on the things you like about yourself; they can be physical attributes or aspects of your character. This daily affirmation of your good qualities will have the opposite effect to these bullies' negative ones. Make a habit of saying positive things to yourself in your mind. By controlling your negative thoughts and replacing them with positive ones you will regain your previous levels of confidence and self-esteem.

23 Is university always the best option?

My mum and dad have always told us that to get on in life you need to finish school and then do a university degree. My older sister ignored their advice and did a hairdressing course. She now has her own business and it's really successful. I want to do well in life but I'm confused about the best thing to do with my future. I've heard negative things about university degrees. Some people say they are just a way to get massively in debt. I've also heard that they don't really help you get a job. Some of my sister's friends who got degrees still work in the same jobs they did before they started. Who's right and who's wrong – my parents or my sister? Is there any other reason to go to university apart from getting work?

Isma, 15

Alex says

There are no 'right' or 'wrong' pathways to choose when trying to decide what to do with your future. If you choose the academic route and go to university then you need to make the most of it, take it seriously and work hard. University is not a decision to be entered into lightly (as you've heard there are fees to pay) and if you want a degree that will secure your future success, you need to get the best one you possibly can. On the other hand if you want to arm yourself for the job market with a more practical set of skills that will make you immediately employable, then taking a vocational course such as an apprenticeship could be the right way to go. In both cases you will have to work hard and put in the hours. It's really good to see that you're thinking about these questions so early on because these choices are really important and will affect the rest of your life. Your parents are much more likely to revise their ideas of what the 'right' pathway in life is when they see you've made the effort to think things through.

In my case I didn't know what I wanted to do and thought uni would help give me more of an idea. I went to uni to broaden my mind.
Amisha, 18

It's your life and you're the one who has to live with the choices you make.
Fiona, 15

There are other things you can learn at university; life skills, social skills and learning about other cultures — these are unique to the uni experience.
Janie, 17

It happened to me

My sister went to university and my parents wanted me to do A-levels and follow in her footsteps. But when I discussed this with the careers officer at school I heard of other career paths that interested me so much more than studying! The careers officer suggested I do some work experience first to get an idea of the types of careers I might enjoy, so I wrote to local businesses and asked to spend a few days working with them. One of these was a company that restored antique furniture. I worked with them for a week and discovered that I loved it! After that I went online and found out the best way would be to get an apprenticeship so that I could get proper professional skills, and earn a bit of money, too. Eventually I got an apprenticeship in a large furniture restoration company. It was hard work but it was incredibly valuable. I did a 2-year apprenticeship and have just set up my own business. My sister has recently also got a brilliant job after finishing her university degree, so we are both satisfied with our careers even though our paths to them were very different!

Megan, 18

Chapter Three

Mates, Dates & Social Media Mistakes

The dos and don'ts of online behaviour

Social media and mobile technology have changed the world forever. You are the first generation of teens to have so many amazing ways to communicate with each other. Apart from text messages, messenger programs, web forums and emails you also have social networks like Facebook and Twitter (to name but two) as well as all the smartphone apps that are continually emerging.

Social media is a great way to keep in touch, have fun, post pictures from your life and generally extend the social networks you have in the real world. Of course it's important to practise safe behaviour – don't trust everything people say, don't 'friend' everyone just to get a large number of followers, and be very careful about geotagging (location tagging to pictures and updates which can be switched off in your settings). Also while they're fun to be on, some of the apps that allow you to be anonymous and post whatever you like are open to all kinds of abuse. If you're going to be using them be aware that not all users have good intent.

Here are some dos and don'ts for using social media. Please take these seriously – the web is a wonderful thing, but take great care while using it! Remember:

* The internet is forever – if you post something online you can't take it back, and this includes sharing any personal information such as your mobile number, address or any photos of yourself.
* Stick with friends. Adjust your privacy settings so that only your friends can see things you post on your wall and limit those who can send you messages. This is really important because otherwise anyone can take a look at your life in intimate detail without you knowing.
* It's OK if you friended someone because you met them in the real world, but avoid adding strangers to your Friends list because you have no way of knowing for certain who they are. The 15 year old boy you are chatting to may turn out to be someone completely different.
* Be careful with smartphone apps like Snapchat that appear to offer 'disposable photos'. There are lots of ways to override these apps and re-post the pictures to social networks or save them. If you're going to send photos online then make sure you are sensible about it. Don't send anything that could hurt you if it ended up in the wrong hands or visible for anyone to see online.
* Pause before posting. Always take a moment to think how any post you make could affect your reputation, relationships with others or if it could get you into trouble. Facebook may be virtual but it's based on the real world – social media is not a computer game!

24 I find it easier to chat to boys online than in person!

Help! I don't know how to talk to real boys from school. There's a boy I really like at the moment and we chat a lot online, but I get really tongue-tied when I see him in person. When I'm online or on instant messanger I can be fun and chatty and think of loads of things to say including witty anecdotes about what happened at school that day, but the next morning, in real life, I dry up and become really shy! Can you help?

Becca, 14

Alex says

Many people find that it's easier to socialise online than face-to-face, so you are not alone. Perhaps it's because we have the time to compose our responses, don't feel self-conscious in the same way, and can feel confident and in control of the situation. These days we rely more and more on online means of communication, but it is important not to lose sight of the 'real' world, too! It can be scary talking to boys you like at first, but if you have built up a friendship online then hopefully you will know some of his interests. Ask him about these and if he's chatting it will take the emphasis off you and your shyness. A good trick to remember when talking to new people is to listen intently and focus on what they're saying rather than what your reply is going to be. Lastly, bear in mind that the more you practise talking to boys, the easier it gets, so pluck up the courage and apply some of your online confidence to your offline socialising!

25 How can I tell if I'm falling in love?

How can I tell the difference between having a crush on a boy and falling in love? In the past I thought I was in love – in fact with pretty much every boy I've been out with – but now I'm not so sure. I'm starting to think they might have just been crushes. I started seeing a new boy recently and for the first time I think things might be serious. We spend all our time together and I can't stop thinking about him. I don't want to tell him that I love him in case it's not true, but I know I want to say it. Is there any way to tell if you're really in love or do you just have to sort of guess?

Ash, 14

Alex says

Having a crush and being in love can feel similar, but there are differences. You can have a crush on someone without meeting them, whereas love usually involves lots of personal contact. A crush is technically an infatuation – in other words it is superficial. Love is about caring for someone deeply and not just for your own sake but for theirs, too. In general, crushes are one-way whereas love is reciprocated. However, crushes have their uses. Some experts suggest that crushes are a way of experimenting with strong emotions – almost like a rehearsal for a real love affair. Crushes are a perfectly normal part of your emotional development. The key message is: don't rush things with anyone at this stage – when you meet someone you love, you will know the difference.

26 My friends take photos of themselves and share them!

> A couple of girls I know quite well at school have been taking photos of themselves and sending them to boys they like via a picture-sharing app. I've heard that the photos are quite flirty and that the boys are sharing them with other boys, and have even posted them online. I'm sure the girls don't know what's going on. What should I do?

Shereen, 15

Alex says

There are some picture-sharing apps that claim to self-delete the photos almost immediately. However, this doesn't stop some users (perhaps not with good intentions in mind) from saving these pictures on their phones and then sharing them. The makers of a popular picture-sharing app called Snapchat advise that no one should use it to send suggestive or sexual images. The only way to be 100% sure that compromising photos of yourself are not being passed around by other boys at school – or being posted on the internet – is never to take them in the first place. The internet is forever! In this particular case, I suggest having a quiet word with one (or both) of the girls and telling them what you know. Show them this advice if you like and direct them to the social networking advice website in Get Connected! on pages 94-95 so that they can avoid a situation like this in the future.

27 My friends hate my boyfriend. Should I break up with him?

I started seeing a new boy recently. He's really good looking but he's an 'emo'. Most of my crowd are into hip-hop and think emo music is depressing. I don't have a problem with his clothes or music, but my friends keep making jokes about him. I'm getting fed up. Should I break up with him just to get my friends off my back? It just doesn't seem like it's worth the effort if they are always going to hate him.

Mia, 15

Alex says

Being in a relationship can often disrupt your circle of friendships. But at 15 are you ready to do that? While being in a relationship doesn't mean you need to share his fashion sense or musical tastes, it does mean that you need to stand up for him to your friends. Your friends sound quite narrow-minded and a bit unkind. If you support your friends in their prejudice then you are supporting the idea that it's OK to discriminate against someone for the way they dress or the music they listen to. It's your friends' attitudes that need to change, not yours, but if you care deeply about your boyfriend you will need to start being loyal to him and support him when your friends make nasty comments. From your letter it doesn't sound to me like you are ready to do that?

28 I've fallen in love with my teacher!

> This term we have a new French teacher. He's from Paris and speaks with a really cute accent. I think I may have fallen for him. I spend all day thinking about him, writing poems for him and wishing for the next French lesson. All my friends say it's just a crush but to me this feels like true love. I'm trying to find out if he has a wife or a girlfriend because I'm 16 next year and old enough to ask him out on a date.

Siobhan, 15

Alex says

Your friends are right. What you are experiencing is a crush. Some say we experience crushes to get our minds used to being in love when we're older. Many people get crushes over authority figures like teachers or people in the public eye like celebrities. You need to face the facts in this situation and realise that the whole thing is one-sided; your teacher doesn't feel the same. You may be turning 16 next year, but he is your teacher so nothing can ever happen. If a teacher did have any sort of relationship with a pupil he would get into very serious trouble. So put the idea of dating this teacher out of your mind and treat your French lessons as a way of getting ahead in a good subject with a teacher you like and respect.

29 I fancy my best friend's boyfriend. What should I do?

My best friend started seeing a boy who I've had a crush on for the last year. The thing is she knew I liked him before they got together. We even talked about it. I didn't approach him because I was too nervous. It's so unfair of her to have done this to me. I would never have got with a boy that she liked. Would it be really mean of me to try and take him off her?

Katerina, 14

Alex says

If you think it was bad of her to start things up with a boy who you WEREN'T seeing, then how much worse is it for you to try it on with the boy who she IS seeing? I agree it does sound like your friend could have been a little more sensitive in her choice of boyfriend. That said, you can't help who you fall for and neither your friend nor this boy were with anyone else at the time. I would try to learn a lesson from this. In future if you like someone, do something about it while you have the chance. But for now, let your friend get on with her relationship. You'll soon meet someone else and it really isn't worth losing your best friend over a boy.

30 Am I too picky and how do I make relationships last?

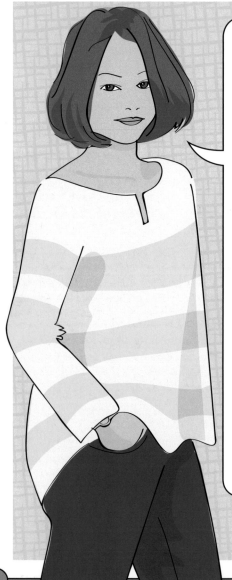

I've always been very picky when it comes to boys. I know exactly what I want and most boys just don't measure up. This means that when I do meet a guy who I actually like, I want things to work out long term because I know how rare he is. My problem is I've never been very good at getting close to people. I'm shy about opening up and one of my boyfriends once called me 'a bit of a cold fish'. I've also been accused of being demanding. I don't think there's anything wrong with knowing what it is you want in a relationship and making that clear. I've just met a new boy who I really like and I'd love to make things work out this time. Can you give me any practical tips on how to make things last long term?

Farah, 16

Alex says

There's nothing wrong with being picky when it comes to boys. Knowing your own mind is excellent and take no notice of ridiculous comments about you being 'cold'. You and the boy who said this were obviously not suited to each other. In regard to the new guy, here are some helpful tips on how to make your relationship last:

It's good to know what you want in a relationship before going into it.
Anya, 15

The best way to get close to someone is to open up to them about your life and to get to know them. This means you need to learn how to listen too!

Someone who accuses you of being a 'cold fish' isn't someone you want to be with anyway. You want someone to respect your feelings and not to undermine them.
Tallulah, 15

Lose your preconceptions of the 'ideal boyfriend'. There is no such thing. Just as you have your own individual quirks, so too will your boyfriends.

Don't lose heart the minute something goes wrong. If you are fond of each other you should try to work through the problems and find solutions to them.

Trust your instincts – it's better to be picky than to get hurt!
Dionne, 16

Be truthful but tactful with one another. During disagreements, try to come from 'I' perspective. For example, 'I feel really sad that we have had this misunderstanding. Do you think there is any way round it?' By coming from the 'I' perspective you are not accusing him, and therefore he won't feel defensive. This can be a more effective way of improving a situation that needs addressing.

Stop looking for perfection. Learning from mistakes is what life is all about. Don't be scared to make them.
Zara, 13

31 I'm always jealous of my friends' boyfriends...

I'm always jealous of my friends and their boyfriends. My two best friends are really pretty and seem to get lots of attention from boys. Both of them are going out with two of the popular, good-looking boys from school. What's wrong with me? I've only dated one boy this year and things didn't work out with him. Why can't I be the one to be happy for a change?

Steffi, 15

Alex says

Console yourself with the knowledge that things are likely to change. Your two friends may be the popular girls right now but this may not be the case in a few years' time. All three of you may change a great deal, both mentally and physically. Boys and the things that interest them will change, too. I know it's great to be the centre of attention but ultimately this is only a superficial enjoyment — true happiness comes from meeting someone who makes your heart skip a beat and who you can build a deep and lasting relationship with. In the meantime, don't worry about what your friends are up to, just relax and start to enjoy yourself!

 **DO** Focus on your own life.

 **DON'T** Let jealousy into your life!

32 Boys are so fickle! Why do they like you one minute and someone else the next?

Can you explain why boys are always changing their minds about who they like? I'm 14 and boys usually ditch me for one of my friends or make up some really annoying excuse about why they don't like me anymore. Is there something wrong with boys in general? Why are they so fickle?

Katy, 15

Alex says

It's a fact that girls mature much more quickly than boys. Teenage boys can be still at a stage where they don't know what they want, when teen girls of the same age can be ready for something a bit more serious. That said, girls can be just as fickle as boys and change their minds about who they like in just the same way! It's all part of working your way through what it means to be in a relationship. In a few years' time everyone will start to become more consistent in their behaviour and you'll probably find that relationships become more long lasting. In the meantime you're doing the right thing by not taking it to heart. You're not doing anything wrong. I would focus on your schoolwork and having a good time with friends for now. In time you'll meet boys who won't change their minds every 5 minutes!

33 He's cheated on me. Should I finish with him?

Leila, 15

> I've been cheated on by my boyfriend –
> twice! The first time everyone at school knew before I did.
> I nearly died of embarrassment. He begged me not to break up
> with me and promised he'd never do it again. Then a few weeks
> later I found out from a friend that he'd cheated on me
> again – this time with a girl from a neighbouring school.
> I have told him I don't want to see him again, but he's been
> begging me to give him a third chance. Do you think
> I should or would it be a huge mistake?

Alex says

Ultimately the decision to trust him again is yours, but you should ask yourself this question: what kind of future do I have with a boy I can't trust? Do you want to be watching your back for the entire relationship? Can you bear the possibility of being humiliated by him yet again? If I really liked someone I might be prepared to give them one last chance, but it really would have to depend on the exact circumstances and only if I thought they were totally and absolutely sincere in their promise not to do it again. Only you can decide if this is what you want but take your time with your decision and don't let him make a fool of you.

 **DO** Take your time and consider your decision.　**DON'T** Allow yourself to be embarrassed a third time.

Sex, Drugs & All That Stuff

Alex says

It's OK to say no...

One of the best things about being a teenager is when you start to have a social life. Making friends and spending time with them is an important part of your development.

However, you need to approach social situations in your teens with some caution and awareness, so this section discusses sex, drugs, alcohol and online gaming. It's good to be armed with information on these things so that you have the tools on hand to be in control of tricky situations.

When discussing big subjects like sex, drugs and alcohol, peer pressure becomes an issue. There will be times over the next few years when the people around you will be doing things that should come with a warning label and you'll need the knowledge, the confidence and the courage to know when it's time to say 'no thanks – it's not for me!'

Alcohol OK, the facts: it's illegal to buy or be bought alcohol before the age of 18. If you drink alcohol when you are young and not used to it, it can be horribly easy to lose sense of what's going on around you. Alcohol lowers your inhibitions and weakens your ability to make sound judgements. You can say things you regret, do things you regret or even get hurt because you misjudge something as simple as walking downstairs or crossing the road.

Drugs There are lots of illegal drugs around now, all with side effects ranging from bad to fatal. Even so-called 'soft' drugs like cannabis are tough on your health, and there is always a likelihood that illegal drugs may be contaminated with other dangerous chemicals. Drugs give you a 'high' (usually followed by longer 'low' state) which is why people take them again – and get into a vicious spiral of need. In a nutshell, resist any temptation to take illegal drugs at all costs. Another thing you need to look out for is that new underground street drugs appear on the scene all the time. These may not yet be 'illegal' (because the law hasn't caught up with them yet) but they could seriously harm you – beware! As a rule of thumb, AVOID DRUGS at all costs!

Sex The age of consent to have sex in the UK is 16. The law isn't there to make life difficult, it's there to protect you. Once you reach the age of consent never feel pressurised to have sex and never risk unprotected sex. Aside from an unplanned pregnancy, this can put you at risk of catching an STI – a sexually transmitted infection. Some STIs can be treated if detected early, but others can have long-term implications on everything from your overall health to your future fertility.

Online gaming Aside from age certification on individual games, there are no specific age rules that apply to online gaming, but you need to be aware that it can be addictive and has been shown to encourage antisocial or violent behaviour in some cases. Stick to the games appropriate to your age and make sure you have a life offline too!

It happened to me

From the age of 14 I've been in rock bands. I've started my own, I've played in other people's bands and I've written songs. I love the friendships that develop when you're working closely with a group of kids who are passionate about something. I formed close friendships with the other girls, especially when we started playing gigs – but there was a problem. One of the older girls smoked and I hated it. My gran died as a result of having smoked all her life and everything I'd been told about smoking just made me feel sick! She didn't suggest I join in, but after a great gig one night, she lit up and offered me a smoke. I realised straight away that it was cannabis because of the unusual smell. I really liked and respected this girl and wanted her to like me, so saying no was incredibly hard but I'm the youngest in the group anyway and I didn't want to be seen as a baby. As soon as I said the words 'No thanks' I was sure my social status had nose-dived. I thought I'd probably messed things up for myself with the band, but to my relief the girl just accepted it. I didn't understand it at the time but it was as if, by being so sure of my decision, I had shown some part of my character that she liked. Since then she hasn't offered it to me again. I'm still in a rock band, I still have friends and I've also stayed true to myself.

Sara, 16

34 I started smoking and now I can't stop!

> A group of us started smoking during breaks at school. I don't particularly like it but it's part of being 'in' with this great group of girls. Now I smoke every day, but my clothes and hair smell and when I had a cold a while back my chest hurt and it took 3 weeks for my cough to go. I know smoking will affect my health more and more, but I'm worried now because I don't think I can stop. Please help!

Nicola, 15

Alex says

You know already that smoking is an awful habit, but did you know that it's also illegal under the age of 16? In the short term it makes you smell bad, it can stain your teeth and fingers and make your skin age prematurely. Longer term it can lead to problems with breathing, such as emphysema or worse, lung cancer. Quitting smoking can seem a pretty daunting task but at your age it's more of a mental obstacle than a physical one. Cigarettes contain nicotine which is physically addictive. When you stop smoking it's nicotine withdrawal that makes you crave a cigarette. The good news is that it only takes two weeks of not smoking for the nicotine to leave your system. What's harder to overcome is the psychological need to smoke. My advice is to visit your GP or local NHS Stop Smoking support service. They can offer you advice on how to stop smoking for good!

35 My friends and I drink every day after school. What can I do?

For the last few months my friends and I have been drinking cider or beer after school. We usually meet up with a group of boys from school on the local sports field. It was fun at first because we used to laugh a lot and I'd work up the courage to chat to some of the boys. Recently though, I worry that it's becoming a habit and could get serious. Last week I was sick on my school uniform and had to hide it from my mum, and another time I fell asleep alone on the sports field and got home at about 9.30pm! I'm starting to wake up with headaches in the mornings and feel sick at the idea of drinking again, but it has become such a part of my social life now that I'm worried if I stopped I wouldn't be part of the group anymore. What should I do?

Janna, 15

Your letter highlights just how easy it is to go from experimenting with alcohol to it becoming a central feature in your life. Being sick and losing track of time from drinking are signs that you need to get help — and fast. Aside from the danger you're putting yourself in, it's worth bearing in mind that no one from the group looked out for you when you were out solate, so you need to ask yourself whether these people are your real friends or not. The reason you feel stuck in this pattern of behaviour is ultimately down to peer pressure. But you can (and should) make a different choice. First tell your parents what has happened and ask them for help. Then make some excuses as to why you can't meet up with this crowd after school for a week or so to break the pattern. Join a new club and generally try your best to mix with a new crowd. There are lots of people you can spend time with whose social life doesn't revolve around alcohol. Who knows, there may be other members of the group who follow your example — so you may not lose as much as you think.

> Pick your closest friend from the group. Be honest with them and see if they feel the same. If they do then the two of you can get out together.
> Lou, 15

> Find some other interests and people to be around. Start a band, play football, get a part-time job — any hobby that gives you something to do will make the difference.
> Jolene, 16

> Drinkers smell bad and look terrible. The next time you see a drunk person ask yourself if that's who you want to be!
> Dominique, 15

36 My brother might be addicted to drugs. What should I do?

Help me, I don't know who else to ask! I think my older brother has a drug problem. I don't want to tell my parents, as I know they'll go mad. I suspect he's smoked weed since he was about 14, and a month or so ago he admitted he takes ecstacy most weekends at the clubs he goes to. But lately I'm worried he might be taking even harder drugs because of some of the things I've seen his friends post on Twitter. The other night I was up late watching a film and he came home and could barely speak. He slumped against the wall in the living room and I got scared. I'm starting to dread the weekends because I never know what kind of state I'm going to see him in. Mum and dad go to bed early so it's unlikely they will ever see him like this! What do I do?

Lilly, 16

Alex says

Your brother is putting you in a very difficult position. I understand that you don't want to get him into trouble but you really need to confide in your parents now, as it sounds very serious. Drugs like cannabis (or weed) are often called gateway drugs because they can lead on to taking stronger ones, so your suspicions could be right. If you are living in a state of constant anxiety and worry, then your brother's actions are not just affecting him but they are making things tough for you, too. Sit down with your parents and tell them everything you know. It sounds like he needs professional help as soon as possible. Show your parents the addresses listed in the Get Connected! section on pages 94-95 for information and help on drugs issues, or they should make an appointment with your GP to get a specialist referral.

I know people say weed is 'soft' but everyone I know who smokes it has gone on to do other stuff. It's just not worth the risk.
Lois, 17

I've seen what drugs can lead to and despite being curious I wouldn't take them – ever!
Phoebe, 16

Tell your parents straight away. I know you're worried about your brother but it's unlikely he'll deal with his problem on his own. He needs help!
Betty, 15

 DO Confide in your parents.  **DON'T** Let this situation get worse!

It happened to me

I started going to unlicensed 'free parties' when I was only 14 because the age restrictions are not as tight as regular clubs, so it was easy to get in. At first it was great; I could dance all night and I met a really diverse crowd of people. I was against the whole idea of drugs and it didn't even occur to me that people were taking them! Over time I realised that most of the crowd I was with took drugs, and, to be honest, it stopped seeming like such a bad idea. It just looked to me that all my friends were having a fantastic time! So one night I took a tab of ecstasy with a guy I knew called Phil. But instead of making me want to dance all night and giving me confidence to chat to people, it made me throw up repeatedly, all over the floor, in front of everyone. I was mortified. Somehow I got home and the next day I told my mum what had happened. She was horrified at first but glad I was brave enough to be so honest with her. Truthfully, I've learned my lesson. It was only the once, but it's an experience I will never forget – and never repeat!

Sylvie, 16

37 Should I stay a virgin?

> One of my best friends at school claims to have lost her virginity. I feel like there's so much pressure to have sex today, but I really don't think I'm ready to take that leap yet. Is it OK to stay a virgin for as long as I like? Or should I just 'do it' to get it out of the way so that I know what it feels like?

Simone, 15

Alex says

The truth is that you (and possibly your friend?) are under the age of consent to have sex and so it would be illegal. But also, think about this sitation. Most girls of your age feel exactly the same way as you do. And there's a possibility that your friend is making it up so that she doesn't look like she's being 'left behind'. At 15 years old it is unlikely that you are ready for the emotional issues that a sexual relationship can bring, not to mention protecting yourself from pregnancy and STIs – this is why the law is in place to safeguard you. My advice is this: you are not ready for sex and that is perfectly normal. It is absolutely the best thing for you to wait until you meet someone you really like. For now, concentrate on being a 15 year old girl – all that other stuff will follow in its own time, and you'll know when it's right for you.

All About Sex...

In our highly connected world, there can be enormous pressures on teens to know about sex and sexuality on the one hand, while remaining safe and protected on the other.

Your body develops at an alarming rate during puberty and as if that wasn't awkward enough, all of a sudden your family (and sometimes your friends) feel at liberty to make comments about your changing body, your height, weight, shoe size, or your developing curves.

As if that wasn't enough to cope with, the subject of sex soon crops up on the horizon, at home, at school, and of course, among your friends. Many teens hate the idea of discussing sex, but let's face it, there are an awful lot of myths out there about what sex is and what it isn't. Some of these myths are downright scary and others can result in you coming to harm or getting pregnant. So reliable sex education in schools, or from your parents, or a recommended magazine or website can be an amazing resource, and advice on sexually transmitted infections (STIs), your menstrual cycle and contraception, is advice that will help you through your teenage years and beyond.

The age of consent to have sex is 16 in the UK, which means that it is illegal for any male to have sex with a girl who is under 16 years of age. But being 16 does not mean that you need to lose your virginity. Ignore people who ask you or tease you about whether you are a virgin or not. It's none of their business. Take your time to meet the right person and having sex will seem like a natural part of your relationship. You'll probably be in love with the guy, you'll feel pretty comfortable in your own skin and confident that you can cope if there's the odd problem.

The issue of whether you are gay or not is one of the most common fears in teenagers. While most of us go on to have a definite preference in our relationships, it can be useful to note that our sexuality is rarely clear cut and our feelings can fluctuate. This doesn't mean that we necessarily will have sexual relationships with both sexes, but that the majority of us are capable of feeling intimate or passionate about both men and women.

Please also remember that when you do reach the age of consent and start having sex, nobody should force you into doing things you dislike or that make you feel uncomfortable. It's ALWAYS right to say no to something that, instinctively, you feel is not right for you. Follow your head!

Remember also, that when you are above the age of consent and start to have sex, you need to practise SAFE sex. Condoms are the easiest to access and one of the most effective forms of protection. They fit over the boy's penis and prevent his semen from passing into your body and risking pregnancy. But condoms are also useful in protecting you from catching STIs such as chlamydia, herpes, genital warts, pelvic inflammatory disorder and HIV/AIDS that can affect your health and fertility.

Sex is a big deal in your teens and beyond, and you owe it to yourself to get the best advice possible. So read on...

 # My boyfriend wants to take things further, but I don't.

Jaz, 16

> I've been with my boyfriend for a year and he wants to take things further. He always tries it on even though I've told him I want to wait until I'm older. I'm happy to kiss and cuddle but I'm not ready to have sex yet. I'm scared that if I don't sleep with him he might find someone else who will. I want the first time I have sex to be special and not because I feel under pressure to do it. I suppose boys do expect to have sex when they're in a relationship, but how do I get him to understand how I feel?

Alex says

What your boyfriend 'expects' in this case is not important, because this is about you! It is your body and this is your decision — and he needs to respect this. If he is putting pressure on you to do something you don't want to do, then he's the one at fault and not you. Sit down and patiently explain your feelings to him and how the pressure from him is making you feel. If he cannot grasp this and he continues to pressurise you to take things further, then it may be best to think about finding someone else who respects your wishes.

 DO Make your feelings clear to him.

 **DON'T** Give in to his pressure!

39 I'm terrified of catching a sexually transmitted infection!

Ever I since we heard about STIs and how dangerous they are in a sex education leaflet given out at school, I've been terrified of having sex in case I catch one! The idea that you can get fatal diseases without knowing about it is also really scary. Why would anyone take the risk of having unprotected sex? How can I make sure I never catch one? Really, it's my worst nightmare!

Bethan, 16

Alex says

The best way to avoid catching an STI (sexually transmitted infection) is to avoid having unprotected sex. This means using a condom each and every time you have sex. Unprotected sex often happens because couples are not prepared, are embarrassed or just caught up in the moment. Make sure you are prepared. The STI chlamydia, for instance, is the most commonly diagnosed sexually transmitted disease in the UK. It's most common in men and women under the age of 25 and you don't need to have lots of sexual partners to be at risk. Other disease risks are genital warts, gonorrhea, syphilis and HIV/AIDS. That said, I don't want you to feel that sex is something to avoid for the rest of your life. You need to know the facts so that you can take action and responsibility for yourself. The bottom line is this: make sure you use a condom when you have sex and STIs are far less likely to be an issue!

40 Can you get pregnant if you have sex standing up?

My older sister's best friend has started having sex with her boyfriend. My sister asked her if she used a condom and she said no, but that it was OK because they did it standing up, which means you can't get pregnant. I've heard people say this before. Is it true?

Nathalie, 15

Alex says

OK, let's put this myth to rest once and for all. If your sister's friend is having sex without a condom she is putting herself in danger not only of becoming pregnant but also of catching a sexually transmitted infection. Whether you are lying down or standing up while having sex it makes no difference whatsoever — sex without contraception can lead to pregnancy. And while we're on the topic here are a few other MYTHS about getting pregnant that you might hear: 'A girl can't get pregnant if it's her first time', 'Showering or taking a bath straight after sex will prevent pregnancy', 'A girl can't get pregnant if she has sex during her period', 'A girl cannot get pregnant if the boy 'withdraws' before he ejaculates'. These are all myths!

41 Should I take the morning-after pill and is it safe?

During sex education at school they told us about all the different methods of contraception. But a friend of mine told me recently that if you have sex with a boy and you don't use anything, then it's OK to get the morning-after pill the next day from the chemist. Is this true?

Cali, 16

Alex says

It's very important to note that the morning-after pill is intended for emergency use only. Using it on a regular basis will disrupt your menstrual cycle (your periods) and is unlikely to work because it's not designed for repeated use. If a girl is sexually active, using a contraceptive method such as the pill or condoms (or both) is the best protection she can get from pregnancy and sexually transmitted infections. Your friend is correct that you can get the morning-after pill from your local pharmacy, your GP or a family planning clinic. They will want to have a chat with you first to find out some details about you, why you have come to need the morning-after pill, plus a bit of your medical history. If you're honest with them they should supply it to you.

It happened to us

I was an idiot. I knew how babies came along but my boyfriend and I didn't use a condom one night (just one night!) and three weeks' later I found out I was pregnant. I ended up having an abortion. It was a totally depressing experience. I know it was the right choice for me but I have really learned my lesson the hard way.

Miriam, 17

I fell pregnant when a condom split during sex with my long-term boyfriend. I didn't go to the doctor for the morning-after pill because I thought it would be just too unlucky to get pregnant. When I started to get sick in the mornings I knew. I was only 16 at the time and far too young to have a baby. I ended up having an abortion. My boyfriend and I are still together, but we don't leave anything to chance now!

Kate, 19

My parents didn't speak to me about sex. I guess they found it a difficult subject and left it for the school (and kids in the playground!) to teach me. I didn't pay much attention in class at that point, I was too busy messing about. When it turned out I was pregnant I was already six months gone. I love my baby daughter now, even though it means I had to scrap plans of going to university and I rarely get to go out. I'm not sure what my future holds at the moment.

Michelle, 18

I'm pregnant at the moment. I chose to get pregnant because my boyfriend and I were in love and wanted to get married. We were only young but I believed in true love. My boyfriend walked out on me about three months into the pregnancy. I was devastated. I'm due to give birth next month and I know that being on my own is not going to be easy. If I could have my time again I would wait until I was in my 20s at least and more settled with a job and a home.

Zoe, 18

42 I'm confused about the issue of abortion. Can you help?

Alice, 14

> I'm confused when it comes to abortion. Some people say it's OK to have one when you have no other choice, like when you are too young to bring up a baby. Other people say it's never right – that it's like murder. My parents believe in a woman's right to choose, but I asked my mum if that meant she would have one and she said no, because she thought it would be on her mind for the rest of her life. I read that there are anti-abortion protesters who stand outside abortion clinics trying to stop girls from going in. I'm not sure what I believe! Can you help?

Alex says

The reason abortion is such a contentious issue is due to the fact that some people believe the cells in the womb called a foetus are already a person. People who believe this are known as 'pro-life' supporters. Then you have people who say that at this early stage the foetus is ONLY a collection of cells with the 'potential' to become a person but this hasn't happened yet. These people believe that given the right circumstances, it's acceptable to halt the development of the foetus BEFORE it becomes a person. These people are 'pro-choice'. Some pro-life supporters can have strong religious views and have been known to protest outside abortion clinics. There are also lots of countries where abortion is illegal, on cultural or religious grounds. As to whether it's OK to have an abortion, in the UK the law says that it's a woman's right to choose, which means you have to make up your own mind.

All my friends go on about sex but it doesn't interest me.

All my friends talk about is sex. I'm worried there might be something wrong with me because I'm really not that interested in talking about it. I told my best friend and she said to be careful because people might start calling me 'frigid'. But I don't care. I think there are better things to do than talk about sex all the time!

Jenny, 16

Alex says

The reason why some people are more interested in sex than others is that teenagers develop both physically and emotionally at different rates. You have every right not to be interested in talking about sex all the time. It is possible that some of your friends are only talking about it to keep up with others? In many ways you are showing your maturity by not discussing something just because everyone else is. Safe sex with a long-term partner when you're above the age of consent (16 years in the UK) is a lovely experience but it's not necessarily something everyone wants to talk about every day.

 DO Stick to what you believe.

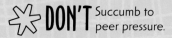 **DON'T** Succumb to peer pressure.

44 Help! I think my sister is addicted to online games.

Dawn, 14

I think my little sister who is 13 is obsessed with a Facebook game. I'm worried because she spends hours playing it alone in her room. She used to go ice skating and see her friends at weekends, but she hardly does either anymore. She told me yesterday that she wants to spend real money in the game and is saving up for it, which is why she doesn't see her friends at the weekends. I don't understand the game, but I'm worried she will lose her friends and interests for the sake of this online game!

Alex says

Online games are not new but have become easier to access due to smartphones. Added to this, the new games that are being developed for them are designed to be habit-forming. The designers of these games want you to come back for more. 'In-app purchases' are designed to swallow money in return for 'exclusive content', which in reality is just pixels on your screen. Have a chat with your little sister and share your concerns with her. Encourage her to see her friends and resume her ice skating by explaining how isolated she may become if she carries on in this virtual world. If this doesn't work, have a chat with your mum and dad (who may not be aware of the situation?) and suggest they limit play time while she is at home. The danger is that online games can consume free time and money, and prevent teens from developing socially and emotionally. Between you and your parents show her some love and support and try to break the bonds of this intense interest before it becomes a full-blown addiction.

45 I have feelings for another girl at school!

> I have strong feelings towards a girl at school. I don't even know her all that well and I'm not sure what this means. I try and spend as much time as possible with her and I find myself thinking about her in lessons when I should be concentrating on my work! Sometimes I wonder if she might feel the same way as I catch her giving me looks and once she made a comment about my hair, which I suppose could mean she likes me. Does this mean I am gay or bisexual?

Aimee, 15

Alex says

It's very normal to have intense feelings and passions for same-sex friends at this age. Knowing for sure whether you are gay or bisexual is only something you can determine over time and it certainly isn't as clear-cut as people think. Different feelings and emotions can take hold in your teens, but take time to get to know yourself and what you like, and if it does turn out that you prefer girls to boys, then so what? The most important thing you should take on board is that liking a friend a bit more than usual doesn't necessarily make you gay. There's no reason for you to worry or to change the way things are with your friend. Just be honest with yourself and see what the future holds.

 DO Relax – and know that these kinds of feelings are normal.

 **DON'T** Put pressure on yourself.

80

Protecting Yourself & Staying Safe

How to stay safe on the street

How to stay safe when you're out and about with your friends is something that is pertinent to teenagers everywhere. There will be plenty of times when you and your friends want to go out, blow off some steam and have some fun together. Bowling alleys, cinemas, friends' houses, cafes, pizza places, youth clubs or under-16s club nights are all popular meeting up venues, but if you're going to be out on your own (and especially at night) then you need to know how to do it safely. Here are my essential tips:

* Put your sensible hat on and, before you go out, plan how you're going to get home! I know this isn't always your first thought as a teenager, but it's good to plan it. Parents, carers or other family members are your best bet here, as usually they will be happy to collect you or arrange for someone else (perhaps another parent) to do so.

* Stay alert and tuned in to your surroundings whether you are walking in the street, waiting for a bus or with a group of friends. If you are walking alone, look confident and as if you know where you are going.
* Always stick to well-lit roads and avoid short-cuts through wooded areas, car parks or alleyways.
* Look out for one another. If you need to leave early let your friends know so they don't worry about you. If you cannot get a lift from a parent or friend's parent, make sure you have a number to hand of a reliable taxi company. **Never** get into an unlicensed taxi and never let a friend get into a cab you've hailed on the road on her own. Anyone can pretend to be a cab driver.
* Don't leave your bag unattended at any time. Take a small bag you can sling around your body and keep with you all the time. Don't leave any drinks unattended either, in case someone has the idea to put something into it, such as alcohol or another drug.
* Keep your mobile phone out of sight as much as possible, particularly on the street or on public transport.
* Never accept a lift home from someone you don't know or from someone you suspect has been drinking. If you're stuck, make sure you call a family member or someone you trust to help you out.
* Trust your own judgement. Don't let other people persuade you to do anything or go anywhere you don't want to. If something or someone makes you feel uneasy, try to leave the situation as soon as possible. If you feel deep down that something is wrong, go with your 'gut instinct' — as that is usually right.

Some of these things sound like common sense, but it's easy to forget when you're with friends and having fun.

46 My Facebook was hacked and I don't know what to do!

I logged into Facebook the other day to find that my password was no longer working. I looked up my profile page and discovered someone had been using my account and posting horrible status updates on my page and nasty things on my friends' pages. Several of my pictures had been deleted and replaced with pornographic images! I'm so embarrassed because people from school will have seen them and I'm worried they might think I did it. What should I do?

Marni, 14

Alex says

It is distressing to feel that someone has masqueraded as you online and you have my sincere sympathy. A Facebook hack is often the result of a stupid 'prank' by a 'friend' (you may have left your profile logged in somewhere). Or it could be the work of a malicious and/or immature hacker who thinks it's funny to create havoc in your life. To regain control of your account, you need to contact the Facebook administrators. Visit www.facebook.com/hacked and follow the onscreen instructions. Once you have regained control of your account the first step is to create a strong password containing numbers, upper case letters, lower case letters and special characters like the @ symbol, for example. In the meantime, explain to your friends that you were hacked and that you are dealing with it. Hold your head up high — you've done nothing wrong!

47

My parents say I'm too young to go to out at night!

I'm 14 years old and all my friends are allowed to go to house parties or under-16s club nights. The club nights are alcohol-free and I really want to go, but my dad has refused and said I'm still too young. I don't understand how I can be too young? I'm under 16 – and in 2 years' time I'll be too old!

Leila, 14

Alex says

It's clear that your dad is anxious about you going out at night. While your reasons for wanting to go to house parties and under-16s club nights are perfectly reasonable, your dad is almost certainly aware of the potential problems and he is trying to prevent anything from happening to you. It would be a good idea to sit down and talk to him and try to reach some kind of compromise. Would he be willing to take you and pick you up from a club night, as much of the trouble tends to happen outside these clubs? Failing that, perhaps you could agree to him letting you go by your next birthday? Build up his confidence in you by sticking to his rules for a while so that in time he might feel that these clubs are suitable for you. Good luck.

 **How do I deal with sexist or rude behaviour on the street?**

> I really hate some of the attention my friends and I get on the street. Aside from older boys shouting rude things to us, I've had boys try to hassle me for a date or even try to grab or touch me.! I hate it but I don't know what to say as they make you feel stupid if you tell them to stop. It makes me feel quite scared and puts me off going out at night.

Polly, 14

Alex says

For some reason certain people think it's perfectly OK to harass teenage girls (and women of all ages) and shout sexist comments and/or grab them on the street or in other public places. The best solution to this type of behaviour is to be firm without being too aggressive, so there is no risk of it turning into something bigger. For instance, say 'No!' loudly and confidently if someone tries to grab at you and ask for help from friends or a passer-by if they won't stop. The important thing here is not to let this behaviour make you feel too frightened to go out. Confidence comes from facing what's happening and talking about it to your friends and family, not hiding away from it.

 DO Say 'No!' in a firm, loud and confident voice.

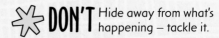 **DON'T** Hide away from what's happening – tackle it.

49 I'm scared of a girl gang who say they want to fight me!

Amba, 15

Near where I live there is this gang of older girls who all hang out together. Whenever I walk past they shout comments about me or my sisters. Usually I ignore it but it's getting worse. I heard from a friend that the main girl in the gang wants to fight me and I am terrified. I am not the fighting type and I am worried she'll start something as I walk home from school. What do I do?

Alex says

Tell someone what's going on now before it escalates. Start with your mum, if that's possible. Tell her you're afraid and that they are picking on you aggressively. Then you can decide together what you're going to do next. Do you want to get the police involved or try other tactics first? For instance, is there another route you could walk to avoid them, and is there a way to make sure you're never alone when you're near them? All these things can stop a confrontation and help you to feel safer when you're out and about. If these things don't work and the abuse escalates or turns physical, ask the police to intervene and stop these girls from harassing you. It can also help to do self-defence classes, not to learn how to fight (these classes are about the very opposite of this) but because learning how to defend yourself can make you feel more confident and in control when you are out on your own. Contact your local leisure centre for details of self-defence classes in your area.

50 He's invited me back to his house. Should I go?

I've been meeting up with this boy every day after school. We've kissed but that's all. He is good looking and I really like him, but yesterday he asked me if I wanted to go back to his house. I said I'd think about it but I don't know what to say. I'm worried he expects me to have sex with him, but I don't feel ready to do this with him (or anyone else) just yet. I don't want to lead him on by going back to his house if this is what he is expecting. But maybe he's just inviting me back to meet his mum? What do you think?

Kiran, 15

Alex says

As you say, his invitation could be an entirely innocent one. His intentions might be to get to know you a bit better by introducing you to his parents, inviting you to dinner or showing you his house. However, as a rule of thumb I think I'd be wary of this sort of invitation. There's always the chance this is a veiled request to take things further. You are below the age of consent for sex in the UK and you have made it clear in your letter that you are not ready to take things any further. Next time he mentions it, try to find out from him what kind of invitation it is and casually ask if you can meet his parents. If he says you'd be alone in the house, then politely refuse his request. You don't have to explain yourself to him. It's your body and your life and you have the right to say 'no' at any time.

51

Boys at school make rude comments about my body!

Ellie, 14

Since starting my new school I've been getting lots of personal comments from boys. Sometimes they are quite insulting, and it makes me feel like curling up with embarrassment! The other day a boy made a rude remark about my chest and I told him to get lost. But then instead of leaving me alone he got really aggressive and started calling me names and saying I was 'easy'. I went home from school that day in tears and told my mum I had a headache the next day just so that I wouldn't have to face him again. What should I do in this kind of situation?

Alex says

Making uninvited and obscene remarks about someone can be classed as sexual harassment or sexual bullying. Unfortunately it is quite common in schools but if you report this behaviour, it will be taken extremely seriously. You did the right thing by making it immediately clear that you found the remarks unacceptable. However, when the boy refused to leave you alone and instead became aggressive, that was the point to speak to a parent, teacher or school counsellor. I know there is a negative perception of people who 'tell tales' in school, but when it comes to something as serious as sexual harrassment you need to speak up and get someone in authority to tackle it. If this boy thinks he can get away with talking to girls in such a way, he won't just stop with you.

52 People call me names because I have lots of boyfriends!

> I go out to the shopping mall most weekends with my friends and we often meet new boys. It's not serious – we just have a laugh. The problem is that some people at school have started gossiping about me and saying that I'm a 'slut'. I think it's really unfair. When a boy meets up with different girls, no one thinks anything of it – so why is it different for me?

Skye, 14

Alex says

All teens (both boys and girls) go through a phase of going out with different people and it doesn't make you a 'slut'. It's basically how relationships work when you are young. What's at play here is a nasty double standard about what is right for girls and what's right for boys. You need to decide what is best for you and what makes you happy. If you can ignore other people's reactions then fine, but if they are upsetting you, you should do something about it and make a stand, perhaps by challenging the people who are calling you names and asking why they think like this. I suspect jealousy is at play here, so the other option is to try to keep your private business to yourself. You and your friends know the truth and that's what really matters.

 **DO** Ignore double standards.

 **DON'T** Listen to gossip; you know the truth!

Alex says

As an agony uncle it's my job to offer advice and solutions to a whole range of problems. When you do this for a living, it's easy to forget that life is full of good bits too. I have included each of the problems in this book as a guide so that in a worst-case scenario you have the knowledge and tools you need to manage these problems effectively – and then get on with your life! Yes, the teen years may be the most confusing time of your life, but they can also be the most thrilling and memorable years when the world is new and exciting, you are meeting new people and having lots of new experiences. I wholeheartedly hope you enjoy every moment of your teen years and I hope this book helps to solve some of the problems you might meet on the way!

Glossary

ABORTION is a medical procedure that is used to end (or terminate) a pregnancy.

ADDICTION is a strong and harmful need to have or take something, usually a drug of some sort.

ANOREXIA is a mental condition that distorts your body image so you still see yourself as fat even if you are normal or underweight.

ANXIETY is a feeling of worry or nervousness that can range from mild to severe. At its worst anxiety can cause panic attacks.

APPRENTICE is a person who learns or trains for a job or skill by working for a fixed period of time.

BENZOYL PEROXIDE is a chemical substance that is present in some over-the-counter and prescription spot treatments that is often highly effective in clearing the skin of spots or acne.

BEREAVEMENT is a time of sadness when a close friend or relative dies.

BEREAVEMENT COUNSELLING is offered to those who cannot cope with grieving when someone dies.

This special type of therapist can help you talk through your distress.

BI-POLAR DISORDER is a mental condition in which sufferers tend to experience intense mood swings between elation and misery.

BISEXUAL(ITY) usually means feeling attracted to people of either sex.

BODY-MASS-INDEX (BMI) is a measure of how much fat your body is carrying for a person of your height.

BULIMIA is a mental condition where there is an obsession with losing weight. Bouts of overeating are followed by fasting or making yourself sick to purge the body of calories.

COGNITIVE BEHAVIOURAL THERAPY (CBT) is a talking treatment for psychological problems such as anxiety and mild depression.

CYBERBULLYING means bullying someone by text, on social media sites, via Twitter or any other app.

DEPRESSION is a state of low mood that can affect a person's thoughts and behaviour. Depressed people may feel sad, anxious, negative and empty and may be unable to focus or concentrate on daily tasks and activities. Depression can be mild through to severe. Medication can be prescribed for depression, these are called anti-depressants.

FOETUS is an unborn human being growing in the womb in the later stages of development. A foetus develops from an embryo.

GAY usually means loving someone of your own sex.

HIV/AIDS are two different things. HIV is a virus that causes your body to attack itself and can prove fatal. AIDS is the range of illnesses you may develop if you get HIV. Two ways of catching HIV are sexual contact and sharing dirty needles to inject drugs.

INFATUATION is a strong passion or interest in someone that is not reciprocated.

MORNING-AFTER PILL is an emergency form of contraception, which needs to be taken within 72 hours of having unprotected sex.

PEER PRESSURE is the expectation that you will copy or be influenced by the behaviour of your friends.

SEBUM is an oily substance secreted by glands in the skin to keep out water and germs.

SELF-HARMING or 'cutting' is the practice of hurting yourself in order to focus your anxieties and obtain temporary relief from severe mental confusion.

SEXUALLY-TRANSMITTED INFECTIONS (STIs) – are infections you can catch from contact during sexual activity.

VIRGINITY means you haven't had sex and your hymen (a thin piece of skin over the entrance to the vagina) has not yet been stretched or split.

VOCATIONAL COURSES prepare you to do a specific job in life, such as becoming a surgeon or priest rather than giving you a general education.

Get Connected!

Here is a list of my recommended help agencies:

Sex & Relationships

4YP Bristol
www.4ypbristol.co.uk
Offers advice on relationships
and contraception.

Ask Brook
www.brook.org.uk
Helpline: 0808 802 1234
Offers contraceptive, sexual health
and abortion advice for under 25s.
The website offers an online clinic.

Staying Safe

Childline
www.childline.org.uk
Helpline: 0800 11 11
Offers 24-hour help and advice on
all issues related to a child's welfare.
Calls are free and don't show up on
a telephone bill so cannot be traced
back to you. There is also an online
chat facility called 1-2-1. To get this
you need to sign up via the website.

Thinkuknow
www.thinkuknow.co.uk
Check out the 11-16 section for
information about online issues from
chatrooms to gaming.

Online Safety

Chatdanger
www.chatdanger.com
This site offers you advice on how
to stay safe online.

Bullying

Bullying UK
www.bullying.co.uk
Deals with all types of bullying,
including cyberbullying. Offers a
chat facility online.

Kidscape
www.kidscape.org.uk
Helpline for parents:
08451 205 204
Advises on bullying and child sex
abuse issues.

Alcohol Problems

Alateen
www.al-anonuk.org.uk/alateen
020 7407 0215
Set up for teenage relatives and friends of people with alcohol problems.

Drug Problems

FRANK
www.talktofrank.com
Helpline: 0300 123 6600
Friendly, confidential 24/7 drugs service with access to live chat and email via the website and SMS (text) 82111.

Gay & Lesbian

Lesbian and gay switchboards
Type 'lesbian and gay switchboards UK' into Google and include your district to find a help service or therapist nearby.

LLGS (London Lesbian and Gay Switchboard)
Helpline: 0300 330 0630
(10am to 11pm only)
Although 'London' is in the title the helpline offers advice across the country on gay, lesbian, bisexual and transgender issues.

Eating Disorders

Beat
www.b-eat.co.uk
Youth helpline: 0845 634 7650
Provides help and advice for people with eating disorders including anorexia, bulimia, binge eating and compulsive overeating.

Local Counselling Services
Most local authorities (your local council) offer youth advice and help. The easiest way to find out what is available in your area is to search the name of your local authority and the words 'youth service' on Google.

Get Connected App

www.getconnected.org.uk
0808 808 4994
Text: 80849
Offers free confidential access via its smartphone app to subjects including bullying, depression, relationship problems, self-harm, suicide, pregnancy, sexual health, abuse, addiction and school issues. Download from the website. Available for both IOS and Android.

Index